West Country Faerie

How and where to see Nature Spirits

Diana Mullis

Bossiney Books • Launceston

For my dear mum

This reprint 2010
First published 2005 by Bossiney Books Ltd
Langore, Launceston, Cornwall PL15 8LD
www.bossineybooks.com
Copyright © 2005 Diana Mullis
All rights reserved
ISBN 978-189938375-7

Acknowledgements
Cover illustration by Patrick Gamble
Photographs by Paul White
Printed in Great Britain by R Booth Ltd, Penryn, Cornwall

Introduction

I have written this book because, quite simply, I believe in faeries. I have done ever since I was a small child. My life, like that of many others, has been a maze of challenges and quests, but what has remained unwavering throughout has been my spiritual faith, my belief that other worlds exist within our wonderful Divine universe.

As a youngster I used to go off into the woods and tell stories to my dolls about the faeries there. I conducted ceremonies to let the faeries know that I wanted to understand them – subconsciously I was honouring their presence. My parents were always open to my mystical wonderings and, although I was a solitary little girl, never once can I remember being accused of being strange.

Stepping aside from social conventions is a risk I've always been happy to take, as it allows me to be my own person in my search for the deeper meaning to life. Today faerie has become such an integral part of me that I consider it present in everything I do.

There has been only a split second of time when I felt I was on a ridiculously empty path. In 2004 I was told I needed a mastectomy to prevent cancer invading my body. Whilst looking out of a friend's bedroom window during what was one of the longest and loneliest nights of my life, I pronounced to the world, 'What a load of rubbish!' In that moment I became even emptier than I ever thought possible. I denounced my own soul and it felt awful. But then the garden in front of my eyes suddenly shone with such luminosity, as the brilliance of a strong moon's light brought everything to life, that I was once again left in no doubt whatsoever about my very special spiritual connection with the faerie realm.

In writing this book I run the risk of provoking adverse criticism from sceptics and disbelievers, as do the beings I represent. But I bring to mind W E Butler, a 20th century esotericist, who suggested that anything found not proven should be investigated with an open mind. I hope you'll adopt a similar attitude and explore the chapters ahead of you with a great deal of enjoyment.

What is faerie?

In order to be clear about what 'faerie' is, I will briefly discuss its two meanings separately.

Firstly, a 'faerie' as an individual is a spiritual being, nature spirit if you like, with an identity of its own. Faeries may reveal themselves in whatever way is most comfortable for you – their nature, appearance and personality may well be unique to your imagination or belief system. So a faerie may to one person be a Tinkerbell with gossamer wings and a sparkly wand, and to someone else it may be a face in a tree trunk, with a gnarled nose and craggy features.

Having said that, be aware that Tinkerbells really belong to fairy tales and pure fantasy (I use the spelling of *fairy* here to distinguish between these literary figures and nature spirits proper). They were invented as a form of escapism by the Victorians who introduced the harmonious flower fairy, and the fairy godmother, to create a perfect world for heroes and heroines undergoing hard lessons on their arduous journeys through life.

I don't wish to belittle this attractive image which many people still cherish from childhood, especially if it keeps faerie in humanity's consciousness, but on the other hand if we continue to reinforce it we merely perpetuate an old-fashioned, incorrect concept of faeries. We need to search beyond the stereotypes, deeper within ourselves for the truth. This book will help shed light on the real essence of these extraordinary beings who exist all around us as well as, if we allow them, in our own psyche.

Secondly, the generic term 'faerie' embraces the whole of the faerie realm, its inhabitants, culture and enchanting mystery. This realm belongs to 'the Otherworld', a spiritual dimension beyond our human existence which is reachable through meditations and visualisation. It can also be explored through study of the great western mystery traditions, something I could not do justice to within the modest scope of this book, so I will not try!

Hound Tor from Greator Rocks. This was a medieval village site, so the land between the tors was once tilled, possibly disturbing any faerie presence.

However, nowadays this area of Dartmoor is carpeted with bluebells in the Spring, suggesting faeries have returned

However, you can easily access the faerie beings of this other-worldly ethos yourself by taking a quiet walk in the woods or on the moors, or even making a recce in your own back garden. Simply using your understanding of nature's elements can help bring into your current reality what may have lain dormant in your being since childhood.

The elementals

In the 16th century a Swiss alchemist, Paracelsus, first coined the term 'elemental' to refer collectively to the various nature spirits living within each of the four elements: earth, air, fire and water. They may be given different names in different countries, but essentially they are the same types of being all over the world.

If you wish to communicate with faeries, the easiest way to start is by being open to them in their own domain. Try visualising those parts of nature represented by these elements and imagine what sort of spirit might live there. In the caves, forests and great stones of the earth you will find the gnomes. This is the family of faeries which include elves (widely accepted as top of the faerie hierarchy), dwarves, hobgoblins and pixies (or piskies as they are known in the West Country – see page 13). Apart from the elves, who are very beautiful and have great presence, to our perception gnomes may be as ugly and deformed as the twists of nature can conjure up, and they tend not to have wings. The wee man who appears on the front cover of this book has neither wings nor glitter. He is of the earth and glows only because of his wisdom and otherworldliness.

Gnomes may take on a leafy, woody appearance and blend into their environment much as a chameleon camouflages itself against the bark of a tree. The tree dwellers, dryads, merge so completely with their home that only a gape of the mouth or a wink of an eye will reveal them to passers by aware enough to notice. But remember that nature spirits choose their homes, much as we do; not every tree, flower or blade of grass will necessarily have a faerie presence.

A desire to see faerie beings can be rewarded by wandering through the countryside, perhaps meandering in meadows looking for and feeling any change that takes place along the way. A sighting out of the corner of your eye (our peripheral vision is often where faerie is seen) could be as subtle as a bend in a blade of grass, a hidden face in a fallen tree or a strange protuberance in a boulder. These are the places where the gnomes live – watch out for them.

The winged creatures belong to the element of air. These are the sylphs and they are closer to humankind in appearance than any other faerie being. They are inclined to have wings in order to survive in their more ethereal element. Their wings however are not necessarily used for flying, but are a collection of energy massed in the centre of the body, known as the heart centre. This energy emanates from the back and looks much like an aura that surrounds a human being.

Insects are often connected to faeries – a sylph, for instance, might decide to ride a dragonfly or 'shape shift' into a glorious iridescent blue insect to avoid detection. In the West Country an ant could be what is known as a muryan, in other words an earth faerie in the final stages of its life before it passes over into even deeper otherworldly realms. So be careful never to tread on an ant in case it is an ancient faerie needing to be left alone. It may surprise you to know that faeries are not immortal – they only live as long as their hosts – and eventually do die. You can therefore see how important it is that we look after their and our environments.

Dragonflies are also associated with the element of water. In the same way the insects hover and dive amongst the water plants and crevices of streams and rivers, so do the undines – the fresh water and salt water faeries, such as Charles Kingsley's 'water babies'. Undines can be seen as sparkles of light glistening within the drops of a waterfall or as the mighty ocean sea mares riding the waves and helping eager surfers 'catch a big one'.

Other water faeries include mermaids, about whom there are many legends. They swim off the shores of Devon and Cornwall, and they are related to the mysterious sirens who are said to lure poor sailors and fishermen to their doom with their exquisitely beautiful singing and enchanting music. (In the north of England selkies disguised as seals are considered to swim close to the land.)

Having been abused and forced into hiding for centuries by an established culture wishing to eradicate them, because of the threat they might pose to formal religion, the faeries are now courageously

A longstone or 'menhir'. Faeries remain where our ancient heritage survives. I once saw a moth about 8 cm across so totally camouflaged against a menhir that I took it to be of faerie

returning to help human beings live in harmony with nature once again. They actually want us to ride the waves, walk the forests and search the floorboards of our homes looking for them – as long as we respect their ways and treat them honourably. This is particularly the case with the salamanders whose element, fire, should always be treated with care. If you've ever watched an open fire in a room or a bonfire, you'll know how the flames dance, and change colour and shape. The salamanders who live in them do just the same.

A salamander (the name means 'hearth') is as big or as small as the

The sirens are said to enchant sailors by their singing and lure them into their caves under the sea

host in which it exists. If the spirit of a candle is small, imagine how vast the great spirit within a volcano must be. It's much less likely to be extinguished easily and illustrates how formidable faerie can be.

Traditional faerie tales reflect this aspect to some degree, as well as comment on the harsh realities of life for human beings. They serve as reminders for us to live as best we can. Famous psychologists have studied the deep meanings and threads of these stories from all over the world. Are they still relevant today – is faerie something to be tapped into when we need to escape or can we embrace it to learn more about ourselves and each other? I like to think that more and more people will wish to do the latter.

Ancestral faerie and its origins

Faerie is indigenous to West Country culture, and our ancestors communicated with faeries all the time. There are tales of wise women or cunning folk who asked them for help with medicines and remedies, and in return honoured the great Celtic festivals and celebrated the seasons. The beginning of Spring, Mayday and Midsummer were and still are important times for the nature spirits who, like the local people, dance and sing, and enjoy the bonfires heralding the change of a season.

The tradition of faerie existed of course long before people from ancient tribes began journeying to West Britain from central Europe. Its origin is lost to us, as it started when stories were handed down orally from one generation to the next. In historic terms the Celtic understanding of faerie is relatively modern and we should always remember that the earth is ancient and faerie spirit has been with it since time began.

In Irish legend we find the clan or tribe of Dana, in Irish the Tuatha Dé Danann. It was said to be a magic-working tribe. Their main stronghold was in Ireland but they spread along the western parts of England, Wales and Brittany. Interestingly, the greatest number of myths and legends associated with faerie come from these areas, perhaps a legacy of when the Tuatha Dé Danann fled into the hollows and hills to escape the marauding armies of the Milesians. They became known as the Sidhe (pronounced 'shee'), the Little People, the Kindly Ones or the Good Folk; it is from this lineage that the West Country piskies, spriggans, knockers etc grew.

There is an element of faerie in the medieval tales of King Arthur, and his sister Morgan-le-Fay. 'Fay' comes from the Latin *fata* meaning The Fates, whilst the Scottish word 'fey' means 'doomed'. But here it probably represents the French *fée*, fairy-woman. The tales of sorcery and magic are woven through the great Arthurian myths: their origin seems to have been in Brittany but they became popular all across Europe.

In the western mystery tradition (whose secrets are only now beginning to be revealed), it is thought that in the year 1113 Arthur became a heroic faerie and heralded a new era that is recognised today by those following faerie lore. It is also felt that Arthur's sister, of faerie blood, was a High Priestess of Avalon (Avalon was considered a portal to the Otherworld) who practised the occult arts and was able to move between realms.

Today for many people Tintagel is still a focus for the rather enigmatic figure of Arthur. Wherever positive human thoughts are concentrated on a particular area of land, faerie will flourish – so visitors to north Cornwall can, if the mood allows, intuit nature spirits whilst walking the rugged cliff paths near Tintagel or strolling through the mysterious woods of St Nectan's Glen and around Rocky Valley.

The romantic faeries of medieval times were said to be human in stature and to covet men's and women's relationships, often enchanting mortals into marriage. Medieval and later Elizabethan literature more often than not portrayed them as beautiful rather than monstrous. By the Jacobean period all connections with the Irish Sidhe had disappeared and now faerie was represented by diminutive beings which, as time wore on, continued to grow even smaller and prettier. These images were a far cry from the truth, but people felt safe and comfortable with them, and it is not surprising that Tinkerbell eventually evolved onto the scene.

Nowadays, with the growing interest in embracing and developing wider religious and spiritual beliefs, including second sight, faerie and the old traditions are undergoing a revival. Thankfully we are now going beyond centuries of fairy tales into the world of real nature spirits where ancient folklore has its roots.

In some countries faerie belongs solely to the shaman who, with the aid of hallucinogenic substances and trance-inducing conditions, traverses the spiritual realms. This is most certainly not to be recommended to the lay faerie worker! In time anyone can have equally valuable experiences, perhaps by means of visualisation alone. All that is required is good intent and respect. Many children know about this – those who have what is dismissed as 'an imaginary friend' are blessed with an awareness which doesn't have to be lost for ever. Adults too can gain a practical understanding of faeries through building a very tangible and meaningful relationship with them.

Becky Falls, near Manaton on Dartmoor. Running water and boulders provide a perfect playground for undines

Traditional folklore faeries

The following are some of the gnome family of faeries that exist in traditional West Country folklore. As part of 'otherworld faerie' they add colour to a belief in metaphysical beings, but they are not necessarily a true reflection of the modern picture. I feel they have been given so many human interpretations that if we are not careful the truth will continue to be distorted by conventional literary stereotypes. So although they and fairy tales form a delightful aspect of an underlying spiritual message, I urge you to view them as a small part of what this book is trying to communicate and to search within yourself to reveal the accurate picture.

Piskies

The piskie is the best-known and best loved of the West Country folklore faeries, traditionally seen sitting cross-legged on a toadstool and wearing a pointed hat and a wide grin. Piskies are thought to be bringers of good luck, and many visual representations of them continue to be sold throughout the south west today. In the past lucky piskies were carried in pockets and purses. Originally made in brass, such charms adorned people's homes as ornaments or doorknockers, were hung on bracelets or were carried loose.

However, the real character of this special faerie friend is not in keeping with its benevolent reputation. Known as the piskie in Cornwall, Devon and Somerset (in some parts it is also called the 'pigsie'), and the pixie outside the West Country, its name is a derivation of the Irish 'phooka' – Shakespeare's Puck in *A Midsummer Night's Dream* was one such character. Piskies are hobgoblins and belong to the earth element where they dwell on the moors and in other wild places. Even today there are stories of folk being 'piskie led', meaning the Little People have played tricks on them. There have been countless tales of villagers who, though knowing the moors well, have fallen foul of strange paths and misleading directions.

Some people have even been known to hear piskie laughter, from which came the local expression 'laughing like a piskie', or have caught a glimpse of something darting in the shadows. If you ever find yourself in such a situation it's thought best to avert your gaze, as the Little People are offended by stares. There are simple traditional ways of avoiding these antics, however. Simply wearing a coat inside out, a hat back to front or turning your pockets inside out will deter the mischief-makers, and they will leave you alone.

In the middle of the last century local people and visitors alike would avail themselves of a charm depicting the currently less well-known 'Joan the Wad'. She is the Queen of the piskies, and her consort is Jack O'Lantern. Today you can buy a Joan the Wad charm from Polperro in Cornwall where she is said to live.

Many believe that Polperro has always been the only place you could purchase the charms, but my father remembers that when he was a lad in the 1930s his father worked for the Post Office in Bodmin, the then county town. Hundreds of small parcels containing Joan the Wads were collected from St Benet's Abbey in Lanivet, where they were also being made at the time. These were destined for places all over the world and contributed heavily to the post office workload, provoking exasperated moans from my grandad and his colleagues. I often meet older people now who show me their charms purchased during the second world war. Some of them were brought back from the front line by surviving soldiers whose loved ones had sent them out as talismans.

Whenever I speak to visitors who are leaving Cornwall to travel home I suggest they might like to hoot their car horns as they cross the River Tamar as a way of saying goodbye to the piskies who will welcome them back one day. This is something my family and I always do as we both leave and re-enter the county.

Knockers

The knockers are said to be mine-dwelling spirits who live underground, particularly in the very old tin workings of Cornwall, and are considered benevolent. In the past it was believed they helped miners find the best ore as well as protect them from danger by knocking on the ground to alert the men that something might be wrong. I say in the past, because tin is no longer mined in the West Country. The mines lie empty and dormant, and I wonder if the knockers still wait for the tasty morsels that by custom were thrown to them by grateful miners. Even today, whenever a Cornish miner chips ore, whether searching for opals in New Zealand or diamonds in South Africa, he will often throw the 'knob' of his pasty to the knockers in acknowledgement of their help.

Some folklore stories suggest the knockers are the souls of Jews who took part in Jesus's crucifixion. They had supposedly been sent to work deep underground, and became the miners' friends.

Knockers are heard far more often than they are seen. They, like the piskies, belong to the gnome family and survive in the earth element. It could be said that a belief in the knockers by big strong Cornishmen is mere superstitious nonsense, but anyone going hundreds of metres below ground would probably feel better thinking they had a friendly earth spirit on their side!

Folklore was originally passed down verbally through the generations. Fairie stories were an excellent way of making sure the ancient wisdom was kept alive by couching it in an appealing way that people would remember. Perhaps there is more than a remote connection between Snow White's helpers going to work with their pickaxes and shovels and the knockers keeping an eye on miners.

Brownies

Brownies are akin to piskies, but are thought to have stronger connections with people's homes than the land.

Derricks

Originating in Devon and Somerset, these are said to be very small in stature and can be malevolent – if they lead travellers astray, it is through bad intent rather than pisky mischievousness.

Is faerie gold hidden under these powerful rocks at the foot of the rainbow?

Spriggans

These are ugly faeries and, according to 19th century folklorists William Bottrell and Robert Hunt, are the faeries' bodyguard (Hunt also alluded to them as the ghosts of giants in *Popular Romances of the West of England*). They have a reputation for bringing illness and blighting crops.

Spunkies

'Spunkies' in Somerset are the same as 'Will o' the wisp' elsewhere in the West Country. They are said to be seen at night as sharp little bright lights, menacingly dancing over moors or bogs to lure people and endanger them. (Anyone preferring the scientific explanation of this phenomenon, *ignis fatuus* – 'foolish fire' – as the combustion of marsh gas, should bear in mind that fire has its own elemental!)

A few of the West Country faerie families, including the spunkies and knockers, are sometimes described as the unbaptised souls of dead children. There is a school of thought that suggests all faeries are the souls of the dead. To me this is rather macabre and, whilst each interpretation is worth considering and I am open to the wisdom of others, my personal understanding is that there is no such connection between humans and faeries.

Bucca

These faeries have an affinity with the sea, and it is wise for local fishermen to think kindly of them, particularly their king, Bucca-Boo, who will ensure good catches and safe fishing.

Faerie today

We live in a world where events, whether man-made or natural, test our faiths and beliefs. Progress is wonderful, but I'm never quite sure whether we are in fact going in the right direction. This is why, for me, my path follows the old ways: the beliefs of our ancestors and the heritage they have bestowed on us seem to make better sense than pushing ourselves to conform to modern pressures.

In the past people were more in tune with their natural environment than most of us are today. They had to be, due to the absence of the technology we have come to rely on for communication. Watching and listening to the land, the sea and elemental forces, the people of the south west were able to interpret the signs and act accordingly.

The change of the seasons would not only tell them what to do with their crops but how to celebrate, when to work and when to rest. At such times they were also very mindful of the Otherworld, and of the need to communicate with the Little People, if all was to go well. They knew that most faeries work in harmony with human beings, but there were (and still are) malevolent beings best to be avoided and left undisturbed. This is not said to frighten you – just follow the same instincts you use everyday when meeting new acquaintances: if you don't take to someone, human or faerie, think twice about pursuing a relationship with them.

Chûn Quoit in the west of Cornwall, about 5000 years old, was a community ceremonial place. Our ancestors lived in harmony with nature and communication between the realms would have taken place here

For centuries the traditional pagan way of life allowed humans and otherworldly beings to co-exist and it was a successful relationship. People who worked closely with the land needed to be in partnership with the inhabitants of nature for success, thereby creating trust and promoting learning between the two realms. However, in time the Otherworld came to be considered a threat by controlling authorities who viewed as evil any belief in anything other than a single omnipotent deity. Faerie was outlawed and anyone seen or heard communicating with the so-called 'occult' was quickly dealt with. The word 'occult' simply means 'what is hidden', and whilst it denotes mystery it certainly does not relate to all things evil.

Fortunately we enjoy more freedom of thought today, although a belief in other beings is still regarded by some people as heretical or just plain weird. For me, trusting and working with faerie has been spiritually fulfilling, and has not diminished but only strengthened my faith in the great Divine. It has made a real difference to my everyday life; when questioned about my point of view, I answer by suggesting that whereas I know faerie does exist, the scorner does not know it doesn't! The creation of nature and nature's law includes the spirit within it, and that spirit is faerie.

When to see faerie

There are certain points in the day and days of the year when faerie is more potent. The dawn awakening creates a mysterious veil over the earth in which nature spirits appear, before many people invade their world. Their activity is often revealed in remote moorland landscapes, especially around ancient stones, during these early hours. Dewy heather and gorse, natural peat bog and steamy moss mounds where the warm sun first hits the land are also typically inhabited by otherworldly folk.

During the day, activity may cease but it is sure to start again in the evening as dusk approaches. So if you can take a walk on a West Country moor at dawn and/or dusk, you may come across an exciting opportunity to communicate with faerie.

Phases of the moon are relevant too. Literature through the ages extols the full moon as a powerful time for mystery and hauntings. Her magnificence and power can evoke awareness of things outside our normal experience, from magical moonbeams to werewolves, and it's an excellent time to meditate, banish old unwanted habits and ideas, and affirm changes in your life. If you can become spiritually absorbed by the full moon's gentleness and authority, faerie may appear to you. You may notice your mood changes when she is at her peak, but this can encourage greater psychic ability and enable you to see beyond your usual physical boundaries.

This can also happen at a new or dark moon when you might consider renewing tasks and promises, and/or starting new projects and relationships. Like the full moon, it would be an appropriate occasion to ask faerie to come into your life. Place milk or cake in a special place as a gift and invitation, but don't expect a thank you! As an aside, it is generally considered bad manners to thank otherworldly beings. They live in an 'unconditional' world where giving is the norm and where the niceties of 'please' and 'thank you' are irrelevant, so non-existent.

Faeries actually appreciate a commitment to their path much more. I certainly try to refrain from saying 'thank you', but because it is part of our human nature and conditioning to be polite in this way it doesn't come easily to everyone. Think of it simply in terms of communicating with people who have evolved a different culture from ours. Like us, they have codes of acceptable conduct; they undoubtedly both feel and appreciate gratitude but they express it somewhat differently from us.

After you have extended your invitation and/or left gifts, write down any feelings or experiences you have. You may not realise it at first, but you will be rewarded with faerie presence, which you can continue to encourage by leaving further gifts – shells, pebbles or any shiny object are received kindly by faeries. If by chance you find an unexplained trinket in your home or garden, it could be a way of them telling you that they want to communicate with you.

A young man I have met several times often walks to the top of Trencrom Hill near St Ives, Cornwall, and at the stroke of midnight will see faeries. He has explained to me how careful he is always to respect them.

It is easy to offend the Little People (kindliness is a must): there are many folklore tales of men being taken by nature spirits and never being seen again. This may seem to be an extreme reaction favoured by yarn spinners, but it is still important to honour faerie space. We would not enter a stranger's home without first knocking and introducing ourselves. The same applies to the faerie realm. If you feel there are nature spirits present, simply announce yourself and ask permission before you tread in their space, pick their flowers or do anything to their trees.

Some people recommend you don't step into a faerie ring formed from toadstools in case the faeries take you to faerieland where time is said to be very different from ours. Morgan-le-Fay thought she had been gone from King Arthur's court only a few hours, but when she returned her brother asked her where she had been for so many years! Such anecdotes make good stories, but many people in the West Country take notice of the messages concealed within these old tales and live their lives according to faerie lore.

The faerie year

You don't have to be a Celt to believe in faeries, but it may be helpful to have an overview of how and when Celts honour the seasons because they often coincide with faerie activity.

Following tradition, the Celtic wheel of the year starts on 31 October when bonfires are lit, and autumn fruits are eaten and offered to nature spirits as an appreciation of summer's end. This heralds the season of Samhain (pronounced 'sow-en') and is celebrated as the new year. It is when darkness falls on the land, we can rest, nature can sleep until awakened again in the spring, and the veil between the worlds is at its thinnest. Because of this it is easier to communicate with spirits, particularly those of our ancestors and of the faerie realm.

Samhain used to be condemned as a time for black rather than nature's magic and has since become associated with ghouls and ghosts which wreak havoc at Halloween. It is an excellent example of how old customs have been misunderstood and abused mainly through ignorance and fear. The pumpkin, enjoyed by thousands of people all over the world as they carve out faces in the orangey flesh, is a legacy of ancient races who believed the head of someone's body housed their soul. When great heroes or holy men died, even sometimes enemies in battle, their heads were cut off and honoured so that their soul would pass into eternity.

The wheel turns to Yule and celebration of the winter solstice when homes are often decked with boughs of holly and mistletoe collected from woodland. There are a number of plants and trees

Rocky Valley, between Tintagel and Boscastle, in early morning light with a trace of mist in the air – a time of faerie awakening.

Where this flow of water meets the ocean, a few hundred metres from where this picture was taken, the power of the elements is truly felt

faerie deems sacred, and mistletoe is one of them. It was certainly considered magical by the druids, holy men who honoured the spirits of trees, including those of oak and apple on which mistletoe grows. Druids would cut sprigs with a golden sickle and would never let them become soiled by allowing them to touch the ground. Yew, rowan and willow are other faerie trees whose wood is still used to make wands.

I have a number of different types of wand. Some are simply twigs I came across whilst out walking, and which felt right for me to pick

A carpet of 'Hottentot fig' or mesembryanthemum, not far from Lizard Point. Plants are best left alone to avoid disturbing the spirits that may live there, as well as, of course, to conserve the environment

up and later consecrate as a magical tool. Before I take anything from a tree, I always ask permission first. Sometimes this has definitely been denied me. For example, I remember once needing a flowering piece of hawthorn for a Mayday event. May is the only month when hawthorn should be picked but, although the timing was correct and I had made my request beforehand, on this occasion I didn't read the signs and I was badly stung by nettles as I tried to reach into the hedge. This made me step back and look around me. I glanced down at the ground a few metres away from where I was standing and there was the perfect piece I needed. I accepted it graciously.

During winter you can concentrate on the faeries who live in your house. In the West Country, brownies, thought by some to be akin to piskies, are the home dwellers. They like tidiness and particularly dislike a dirty hearth, although this will not necessarily deter them entirely!

The next date of note in the year is 1 February. This is called Imbolc, which means 'in the belly' and represents the period before Spring is born. It is when snowdrops burst on the scene and there is a general sense of the earth becoming fruitful once more. Next comes the Spring equinox (equal dark and light) on 21 March. Known originally as Eostre (later becoming Easter in the Christian calendar), growth and fertility were celebrated by people burying eggs in the ground and, symbolising re-birth, digging them up three days later.

The wheel then moves on to Mayday or Beltane, one of the most popular festivals of the year. In the West Country there is much dancing and enacting of pagan rituals, such as the 'Obby Oss' at Padstow. Faeries love Beltane. They encourage us to dance and sing and have fun, and remind us that while we live on earth as humans we should try to keep in touch with the childlike side of ourselves. Playfulness and innocence are qualities to cultivate. Faeries also help us, spiritually speaking, to keep our feet firmly on the ground.

Angels, on the other hand, are of the heavenly domain and often answer our prayers in a different way. It has been of great interest to me to discover through my work that there are those who believe in angels and those who believe in faeries. Some work with both, but their allegiance is more likely to be stronger with one than the other.

Faeries, I am pleased to say, are 'naughtier' than angels and allow us leniency on our spiritual journey. They certainly have a delightful sense of humour, but will soon show displeasure if we abuse their trust and they do not tolerate bad manners – in their world they have a strict moral code, with high standards, which is always enforced. Their main desire for us is that we are generous, look after

A stone circle and stone row. Faeries would certainly congregate here

the earth and live harmoniously with all creatures; they will help us all they can if we are sincere and do the best we can.

May is considered a sacred month and old custom suggests that it is unlucky to be married during May, as it is a month for faeries alone to celebrate. In contrast midsummer or the summer solstice, falling on the longest day, 21 June, is when the fay, like humans, gather together to share their celebrations.

Standing stones and stone circles are special places, and it's not just the large circles such as Stonehenge and Avebury that attract nature spirit activity. Whatever they once meant to local people and however they were put into place, the standing stones and circles, and even stone outcrops throughout Somerset, Devon and Cornwall (have a look at the Ordnance Survey map for locations), all have special resonances with the faerie realm. My particular favourites are listed on page 40.

Sitting quietly in a stone circle or leaning gently against a large boulder can help create a state of consciousness in which it is possible to communicate openly with nature spirits. If you still your mind and ask faerie to make contact with you, you may experience a change in your awareness which will then allow you to feel their presence. I sometimes ask for a definite sign to confirm that faerie is with me. On one very memorable occasion while walking in a wooded area I did just this and to my absolute joy a stag appeared. When I saw him I knew instinctively that a fabulous connection between the Otherworld and myself had been made. In the western mystery tradition, the stag is a manifestation of the horned god Cernunnos, also known as Lord of the Greenwood and Lord of the Dance. With the onset of Christianity, the horned god was conveniently misrepresented as the devil, but to people following a faerie path he embodies the green of nature (as in the Green Man, Robin Hood and Pan).

After midsummer comes the harvest when faeries and humans are busy. 1 August is the festival of Lughnasadh, named after the Celtic sun god Lugh, during which the earth's largess is celebrated. In the past country folk offered gifts of corn, fruits and grains to faerie to ensure continued abundance (anybody offending the nature spirits could find their crops blighted or their livestock diseased). Today the harvest festival continues to be a form of thanksgiving and harvest suppers maintain the hallmarks of faerie celebration, often with dancing, music and feasting.

The autumn equinox on 21 September brings the year nearly full circle. Although it is not a major festival in the Celtic calendar, it is nevertheless a poignant reminder that winter is coming and a new cycle is about to start all over again.

Where and how to see faerie

As I've already discussed, faeries are more active during the twilight hours, new and full moons and the eight Celtic festivals. But where exactly can they be seen?

For some people it's more a case of feeling them than actually seeing them. For others a sighting can be so vivid that they are left in no doubt that what they have witnessed is not of our world. I myself have had four such experiences in my life. One I will relate here occurred when I was in my late teens. I was feeling very vulnerable and was searching desperately for some answers to my problems.

I was travelling as a passenger in a car and we had been driving through Epping Forest. I remember being unhappy and confused. I suddenly saw a tiny man wearing a red coat and green breeches, who appeared out of nowhere, standing on the pavement. He had one leg crossed over the other, and he was leaning against a lamppost. What struck me as very odd was the broad grin on his face, like the one I always imagine the Cheshire cat having in Lewis Carroll's *Alice through the Looking Glass*. I was quite stunned to see him and I knew instantly that he was not a human being – I thought at first he was a ghost. When I looked again he had vanished.

During my studies into the faerie realm I came to realise that what I had observed was a faerie being. He was in the earthy colours of a gnome (I would expect that, as he was on the edge of a forest) and he was there for me when I needed reassurance. Although I was initially alarmed by his presence, I recall soon feeling safe – something of great benefit to me at the time. I might also add that he did not look unlike the being on the front cover of this book.

More often than not, however, a sighting for most people is quite a subtle affair. I'm frequently aware of what I call 'scuttles' in my peripheral vision. These are quick movements from one corner of my sitting room to another, usually from north to south, and are rather like small brown clusters darting across the carpet. When I look directly at them, they've gone. This type of experience is related to me time and time again by individuals I meet, and the description is always similar to my own. In my case I'm surprised that the scuttles seem to emanate from the hearth – as I mentioned earlier, faeries don't like dirty hearths and I have to confess to not being the tidiest homemaker in the world!

The photograph above shows what I would call a vortex effect. It represents a portal through which Faerieland can be reached. Strangely, turning the page upside down reveals a similar image

We can train ourselves in the art of clairvoyance by meditating and generally stilling our minds and bodies in order to be more receptive to other beings. As we become more open and aware, then our spiritual eyes will develop. If it doesn't happen for you immediately, don't give up: faeries will contact you if they wish to, but they may wait a while to gauge your intent. Communication is a two-way process, and both parties must be willing to make an effort and build up trust. It is so important that we try, because in so doing we will learn a huge amount. Faeries also wish to gain a greater understanding of us, and they will undoubtedly value a relationship with you if you follow your heart's dictates.

Some places are more attractive to nature spirits than others. It's not difficult to appreciate why a wood full of primroses and bluebells or an ancient moorland site are typical faerie domains. But there are more specific habitats which may be less obvious to those unacquainted with faerie ways, as well as signs to watch out for which indicate that faerie is present.

For instance, two trees close together, looking like a pair, create a magical space in which to experience the Little People. Such trees stand as pillars forming a portal or gateway into the Otherworld. There is a perfect example at Carwinion, a garden in Mawnan Smith on the Helford River in Cornwall. Not only are there two straight, tall trees, but they stand on a mound.

Mounds have even greater significance when looking for faerie, as it is thought they provided safe places for the Sidhe, members of the Tuatha Dé Danann, when they were fleeing from the Milesians. Large mounds, usually ancient burial sites or barrows, are marked on maps as tumuli (singular tumulus, from the Latin meaning a heap of earth) and are well worth checking out – beautiful music emanating from them has been reported on various occasions.

In literature there are a number of characters who mysteriously disappeared after being enchanted by faerie music or inadvertently entering Faerieland by stepping on a faerie mound or into a ring of toadstools. Thomas of Erceldoune, also known as Thomas the Rhymer, a gentleman living in the 13th century, was a Scottish seer and poet. He was supposed to have been taken into Faerieland where he became romantically entangled with the Elfland Queen who taught him prophecy. A manuscript of the ballad of this story was discovered in the 15th century (various copies still survive), although it could have been written earlier.

In the late 17th century a highland minister, Reverend Robert Kirk, met a questionable death after risking not just his reputation but also his life by writing what has now become one of the most important reference books on faerie, *The Secret Commonwealth of Elves, Fauns and Faeries*. Not printed until 1815, it warns of the harsher characteristics of faerie, which should be respected, but it also encourages readers to believe in the Otherworld – which Robert Kirk most certainly did. Shortly before his death he disappeared and his body was later found near a mound at Aberfoyle where he was a minister. Locals thought the body was that of a changeling or 'stock' and that Kirk was still a prisoner in Faerieland.

Look for the signs of the Otherworld – such as damp mossy areas, protruding tree roots, and bracken – on your favourite walk or in your own garden. These are the places faeries inhabit in gardens large or small, the secret nooks and crannies you can learn to recognise by tuning in to the environment. You might walk for miles and not experience anything other than an appreciation of the lovely scenery, but then suddenly become aware that you're not alone – that the bark of an old oak tree has turned into a face or grasses are fluttering when there isn't a breath of wind.

A special faerie place I love to visit is St Nectan's Glen, a wooded valley lying between Tintagel and Boscastle on the north Cornish coast. It climbs up to a waterfall and the woods turn blue in May as the carpet of bluebells stretches as far as the eye can see. Bluebells house one of the more malevolent nature spirits. These faeries do not like their flowers to be picked, something our ancestors may have known and passed down to us through superstition: it's considered bad luck to pluck bluebells and bring them into the house.

At the top of the glen the waterfall and pool are tucked into lichen-covered craggy rocks. The water is crystal clear and I feel the faerie presence every time I visit. St Nectan's is used to celebrate festivals, and those attending, or just passing by, often tie little rags or trinkets onto the trees as offerings to the deities and spirits. These offerings which have been made in the same way for centuries are called 'clouties' (pronounced 'clooties') and can be found at many ancient West Country sites – sometimes posies of flowers, shells and crystals are also left around sacred wells and stone circles. Occasionally the 'keepers of the stones', people usually of pagan belief, will clear the sites, but the gifts are always treated with honour and respect, and are buried or placed on a festival fire where the keepers believe the local deities will receive them.

Wherever clouties are left, faeries are sure to visit. It is a way of both sides rebuilding relationships and bridging the divide between the faerie realm and our world. After faeries were condemned as demons, they took refuge in hidden places – caves, water, trees and

'Clouties' attached to a tree over a Holy Well

flowers – and, not surprisingly, were reluctant to communicate with humans in the same way as they had done in the past. However, I believe we are now regaining their trust and that they wish us to co-operate with them so that they may help us bring order to our often chaotic approach to nature.

After the dramatic events of 11 September 2001 in New York, I was approached by many people explaining to me their sudden awakening to the prospect that otherworldly beings exist. This came as no surprise to me, because such upheavals caused not only by loss of life but by subsequent spiritual questioning can bring about great positive change if we allow it to happen. I received letters, calls and visits from people telling me of strange experiences which led them to adopt different attitudes, show more compassion and tolerance to others, and recognise that while life can be very fragile we should

Opposite: A typical faerie landscape. Look for faces in the trees

make the most of every minute we live it. This is just what faerie teaches us – faeries want us to be free-spirited, playful, yet watchful, and sometimes they give us markers to show their support or offer encouragement.

For example, folk coming across white feathers is always of interest to me (numbers of individuals experiencing this phenomenon rose substantially post 9/11). White feathers found unexpectedly out of context can be joyful, very real reminders that spiritual beings are present – to find one in the country near a chicken coop is one thing, but to see one drifting down from a bedroom ceiling is quite another, especially if you sleep on synthetic pillows! Keep an eye open for these marvellous calling cards.

Several years on from 2001 there are now many people consciously working with faerie and thousands more seeking a faerie path. One of the comments I often encounter is, 'Thank goodness there are others like me'. And another common statement is, 'I feel so stupid talking about faeries as if they are real!' Believe me they are real and they need our help as much as we need theirs. So, it is necessary to know where to find them and how to contact them.

To recap: go anywhere you feel you are likely to experience a shift in awareness, somewhere you always enjoy and feel safe. You can create your own small sacred space in your home, perhaps with an altar, or in your garden with a lovely pot of flowers. Or you can go further afield. It does not have to be Rivendell, the city of the Elves in Tolkien's *Lord of the Rings*, though places as magical and mysterious as that do exist. In the West Country there are countless places where it's not difficult to feel surrounded by something special. I am very fond of the enchanted wooded areas at Watersmeet in Devon and Withypool in Somerset. At both of these places I have felt faerie quite strongly.

Unspoilt woodland is a favourite environment for the Little People, but don't take it for granted that such places are always inhabited. It's up to each person to decide for themselves if there is a presence – try to centre yourself and ask from your heart for an acknowledgement. Sometimes it is obvious as soon as you walk into a place that it is enchanted. You may start to shiver and feel the urge to look around you, a sense of peace may come over you or you may be filled with excitement and an inner knowing that you are at one with your surroundings.

You may also receive direct evidence that someone is walking alongside you or 'spying' on you. Martin Matthews, someone I met while writing this book, described to me the time when he was pelted with acorns while walking through Luxulyan woods near Lostwithiel in Cornwall. He wouldn't have taken much notice but for the fact that there were no oak trees anywhere near the route he was walking. He took more notice from then on!

If you ever feel uneasy in the presence of faerie, then I suggest you simply proceed cautiously and with respect. Don't be alarmed, but just understand that not all of nature's spirits are as pretty and gentle as those depicted in the world of Disney. Honour yourself and faerie, and you will be fine.

I find it useful to write down locations and experiences, however fragmented they may seem at the time. Gradually a pattern may emerge or a consistency develop which can suggest a connection is being made. Then it becomes very exciting indeed.

Six years ago I opened my own shop in Truro and dedicated it to my belief in the Little People. I named the shop 'Faerie' and, as tiny as the space was, it attracted a wealth of stories and experiences from people who shared my interest. Amongst the many anecdotes I listened to there were a few which struck me as particularly plausible. I would like to share a couple of them here.

A woman was walking with a friend in woods near Cardinham, Cornwall, when she spotted something that she thought was a butterfly on the bark of a tree stump. She remembers thinking the colour was rather rare for a butterfly and she stepped closer for a better look. As she approached, the creature's bright blue shape took off and moved with 'the speed of light' around the back of the stump. Its behaviour also was not that of a butterfly, and when the

Left: Foxgloves are a favourite with faeries, who use the bells as hats and suck the stamens to make themselves 'merry'. Definitely not advisable for humans because the whole plant is extremely poisonous

Opposite: The White Lady waterfall at Lydford Gorge. An onlooker cannot fail to be overwhelmed by the power of this place

woman checked around the stump it was nowhere to be seen. She and the friend who was with her at the time knew without doubt what it wasn't – a winged insect – and could only come to the conclusion that it was a faerie. I could tell by her expression and the way in which she recounted the tale that she was convinced she had seen a nature spirit and it had brought her great joy.

I have discovered that people who say they have seen faeries, including myself, are always left in no doubt whatsoever about the real essence of their experiences. Those who have not previously believed in such phenomena soon start questioning old beliefs when

they catch sight of something that cannot be explained by modern science.

On another occasion a man on a walk with his family near Wiveliscombe, Somerset, saw movement round the roots of an oak tree, which attracted his attention. He focused his eyes on it and saw the face of a creature that seemed to be part of the tree yet apart from it. Like the lady in Cornwall, he moved closer and the face shot him a startled look and disappeared. The man too was filled with a great sense of joy and trod his path with greater awareness from then on.

I totally accept these accounts, as they describe typical images and behaviour of otherworldly beings. While ancient tellings of folklore captivate our imagination, such recent anecdotes of sightings and experiences from people in the 21st century really bring faerie well and truly into our modern lives.

Traditional faerie lore

There are a number of do's and don'ts when working with the faerie realm. Some originated from folk superstitions, such as always to hang an open pair of scissors over a baby's cot to prevent the child being stolen by the faeries and swapped for a changeling – a sickly faerie newborn. It was thought that a healthy human baby might bring good stock to a faerie family whose own child was less than robust. (A young woman who had felt for some time that she was a changeling approached me a few years ago after I had given a lecture on faerie lore. It was a serious issue for her and one I also could not look upon lightly.)

The fact that an open pair of scissors would more than likely fall and impale the poor infant before ever being seen by faerie seems to have been quite irrelevant to our ancestors. However, their belief was based on a historic theory that faeries don't like iron, possibly because of its association with battles, weaponry, etc. Even today it is still used as a protection against malevolent beings.

Due to the faerie dislike of iron, it is thought they do not tolerate bells, certainly the ringing of bells – the noise distresses them. They also feel insecure in the presence of a Christian cross. This is purely because of the condemnation they received from the Church, and does not mean they are demons. On the other hand, the equal armed cross of Celtic religion, symbolising the equality and balance of the four elements and the four universal directions of north, south, east and west, with Spirit at the centre, is acceptable to faerie. In fact they will often gather at a crossroads, a place which represents for them goodness and wholeness.

Superstition also decreed that dirty socks left under the bed would repel faeries. At the risk of generalising, being sexist, ageist or other '-ist', any unprepared person – faerie or not – visiting the bedrooms of teenage boys can be in for a shock!

Faeries like order and cleanliness. If you create a sacred place in your home or garden, it is much more likely to be visited if it is kept neat and tidy. This can be taken to extremes however: I remember when the new owner of a sacred site in Devon cleared away decades of ivy growth and plant life. By so doing he also cleared away all sense of faerie presence. Let your own instinct be your guide, and in time and with practice you will know what is needed to experience faerie for yourself.

With any prayer said or spiritual desire expressed in a heartfelt manner, I think our chosen deity, teacher or familiar (otherworldly guide and friend) will respond with compassion. They understand our human frailty and we must not get too hung up on spiritual etiquette. As long as our intent is sound and we show respect, I do not believe we incur any wrath. That said, we can benefit greatly by learning about the ways of others. It can only enlighten us and reward our desire to communicate, which is made so much easier and is so much more fulfilling if we all speak the same language.

Some faerie sites in the West Country

Cornwall
Carn Euny (SW 403288)
The Gump, West Penwith (SW 397335)
Heligan Gardens
Kennal Vale Woods, Ponsanooth (SW 752376)
Luxulyan Woods (SX 059573)
Respryn Bridge, near Bodmin (SX 099635)
Roughtor Moor, Fernacre Circle (SX 144799)
St Nectan's Glen, Tintagel (SX 080885)
St Nonna's Well, Pelynt (SX 224564)
Stannon Circle (SX 126800)
Trebah Gardens, Mawnan Smith
Treen, near Land's End (SW 403227)
Trelissick Woods, near the King Harry Ferry
Trencrom Hill, St Ives (SW 519362)

Devon
Bellever Tor (SX 644765)
Fernworthy Reservoir woods, near Chagford (SX 664842)
Fice's Well (SX 577759)
Fur Tor, near Lydford (SX 587831)
Lydford Gorge (SX 506842)
Tavy Cleave (SX 530830)
Shipley Tor (SX 685632)
Watersmeet (SS 744486)
Wistman's Wood (SX 613775)

Somerset
Barrow Gurney (ST 532686)
Blagdon Hill – site of a fairy fair (ST 212179)
Buckland St Mary (ST 271134)
Butcombe – Fairy Toot (ST 520618)
Glastonbury Tor
Porlock Hill, Exmoor – woodland
Withypool, Exmoor
Wiveliscombe – woodland
Weston-super-Mare, Worlebury Hill (ST 325625)